The Environmental Agenda

Taking Responsibility
Built Environment

Written and compiled by
Samantha Woods, *De Montfort University*
with contributions from
Clive Beggs, George Henderson and Peter Moors

A Council for Environmental Education Programme funded by the Department of the Environment, in partnership with WWF (UK)

Pluto Press
LONDON · BOULDER, COLORADO
in association with WWF UK

First published 1994 by Pluto Press
345 Archway Road, London N6 5AA
and 5500 Central Avenue,
Boulder, Colorado 80301, USA

British Library Cataloguing in Publication Data
A catalogue record for this book is available from the British Library

ISBN 0 7453 0930 5 Paperback

Taking Responsibility titles appear in The Environmental Agenda series
published by Pluto Press in association with WWF UK.
ISSN 1353 - 6842

Library of Congress Cataloging in Publication Data
Woods, Samantha.
    Taking responsibility : built environment / Samantha Woods.
       p.   cm. — (The Environmental agenda series, ISSN 1353–6842)
    ISBN 0–7453–0930–5 (pbk.)
    1. Environmental education—Great Britain. 2. Environmental
sciences—Study and teaching (Higher)—Great Britain. 3. Curriculum
planning—Great Britain. I. Title. II. Series.
GE90.G7W66   1995
363.7'007'1—dc20
                                                                94–35060
                                                                      CIP

98   97   96   95   94
 5   4   3   2   1

Designed and produced for Pluto Press by
Chase Production Services, Chipping Norton, OX7 5QR
Typeset from author's disks by Stanford DTP Services, Milton Keynes
Printed on recycled paper in the EC by JW Arrowsmith Ltd

Contents

PREFACE

This publication is one of a series produced as part of the Council for Environmental Education's Education and Training for Business and the Environment programme. The broad aim of the programme is to develop environmental education policy and practice within the further and higher education sector, with a particular focus on the needs of business and industry.

The programme is supported by the Department of the Environment and WWF UK (World Wide Fund for Nature) and stems from the government's commitment in the 1990 White Paper 'This Common Inheritance' to sponsor a series of conferences with a 'market place' function, bringing together industry, educationalists, trainers and course providers.

The publication series is the outcome of a national series of seminars, which took place between March 1993 and January 1994, and an associated national research exercise to identify appropriate environmental content, skills and good practice relating to integration and evaluation methods in 11 targeted educational areas.

This publication is based on the research material drawn in by De Montfort University who also hosted the national seminar on the theme Environmental Education across Higher Education Curricula: Built Environment.

1   INTRODUCTION

1.1   The Project

The Education and Training for Business and the Environment project was formulated in 1992 in response to the 1990 government White Paper 'This Common Inheritance – Britain's Environmental Strategy' which states that:

> The Government will sponsor a series of conferences with a 'market place function', bringing industry, educationalists, trainers and course providers together.

These guidelines represent the outcome of one such conference, looking specifically at environmental education in the fields of the Built Environment, together with the results of a nationwide trawl of existing good practice.

The aim of the project is to facilitate the development of environmental education policy and practice within further and higher education (FHE), with a particular emphasis on the needs and expectations of business, industry and the professions; and to develop in all students the ability to recognise and act on the environmental implications of their personal and professional decisions. The intention of the guidelines is to provide a basic outline of how environmentally conscious personal and professional values can be integrated into built environment courses, illustrated with case studies from higher education and the professions. At the end of the guidelines a list of contacts and resources is given.

The Toyne Report

> There is a long way to go in creating environmental education that will produce rounded citizens, acceptable employees and sensitive policy-formulators and managers fine-tuned to the environmental revolution that has already begun. But that is all the more reason to be making an urgent start on the common task.

This is the conclusion of Professor Peter Toyne in the recently published report to the Department for Education (DE) of the Committee on Environmental Education in Further and Higher Education.[1] The report examines the need for a basic level of awareness across the workforce as a whole to deal with the challenge of responding to such threats as global warming, ozone depletion, acid deposition and the continuing loss of planetary biodiversity. Focusing on the way in which further and higher education should respond to this need within the workplace, the report outlines three major areas of involvement:

i.   specialist courses leading to specific environmental qualifications;

ii. updating courses for those already in the workforce;

iii. environmental education for all students, whatever their specialist areas of study.

The DE report notes the competition that FHE faces from other bodies in providing courses designed to keep the workforce up-to-date and recommends increased communication between FHE and employers. It is expected that the demand for updating will increase as employers become more aware of their own environmental training needs, particularly if/when the smaller and medium-size enterprises follow the example of the larger companies in promoting themselves on the basis of positive green image.

The impetus towards cross-curricular greening has developed from the realisation that environmental issues encroach on all areas of life and that an environmental element is required in all courses, both to meet work-related needs and, more broadly, students' needs as citizens.

It was recognised that 'Greening cannot be expected to develop at the same pace ... in every institution' and that a variety of methods may be used to introduce the required content, but generally FHE institutions and national examining, validating and accrediting bodies must apply themselves far more vigorously to the process than they have done to date.

Agenda 21

Agenda 21 is the international agreement to work towards sustainable development signed by many nations at the United Nations Conference on Environment and Development held in Rio de Janeiro in 1992. Sustainable development has been defined as development which meets the needs of the present generation without jeopardising the needs of future generations.

Chapter 36 of Agenda 21 examines the need for promoting education, public awareness and training to achieve sustainable development. Education is seen to have a critical role to play in improving the capacity of people to address environment and development issues and Chapter 36 stresses the need for the integration of the dynamics of both the physical/biological and socio-economic environment in all disciplines.

A review of existing curricula to ensure a multidisciplinary approach and the building of partnerships with industry and other bodies are recommended, as is the promotion of interdisciplinary research. Agenda 21 emphasises the need for broadening the base of involvement in decision-making at all levels, to bring about the necessary changes to thinking, as well as action, on environmental matters.

Fostering opportunities for women in non-traditional fields and eliminating gender stereotyping in curricula are prioritised elements of improving access to education in general and specifically the new green curricula; particularly relevant to the traditionally male-dominated world of the built environment. The involvement of young people is also particularly stressed.

The National Curriculum
Environmental education is one of five cross-curricular themes identified by the National Curriculum Council; the others being:

• education for economic and industrial understanding;

• health education;

• careers education;

• education for citizenship;

The environmental content of the National Curriculum covers the following:

• the natural processes which take place in the environment;

• the impact of human activities on the environment;

• different environments, past and present;

• environmental issues, such as the greenhouse effect, acid rain, air pollution;

• local, national and international legislative controls;

• how policies and decisions are made about the environment;

• the environmental interdependence of individuals, groups, communities and nations;

- how human lives and livelihoods are dependent on the environment;

- the conflicts which can arise about environmental issues;

- how the environment has been affected by past decisions and actions;

- the importance of effective action to protect and manage the environment.

This provision of environmental education within the schools sector requires an effective response from FHE, where currently the environmental awareness of students is often greater than that of their teachers.

Other Initiatives

Other education bodies have been developing environmental content in courses, either of a cross-curricular nature (BTEC) or specific environmental qualifications (Training Education and Enterprise Directorate).

BTEC has developed a series of environmental learning outcomes relating to:

- environmental responsibility;

- science and technology;

- resource management;

- business practice;

- policy and control;

- investigation.

For each of these a group of environmental learning outcomes has been identified, including some indication of performance criteria and range. Those relating to environmental responsibility are regarded as essential for students on all courses, whilst those in the other areas are regarded as more specialised and dependent on the chosen course. Examples of these are given in the chapter, Integration Methods.

Encouragement from the Training Education and Enterprise Directorate (TEED) has led to the establishment of two industry-led bodies developing vocational qualifications in environmentally related fields.

The Council for Occupational Standards and Qualifications in Environmental Conservation (COSQUEC) is developing National Vocational Qualifications (NVQs) in many areas including building conservation, sustainable resource management and landscape and countryside conservation. COSQUEC's remit extends beyond the conservation sphere into influencing and promoting standards in other relevant occupational sectors.

The second lead body is the Waste Management Industry Training Advisory Board (WAMITAB); set up primarily as a response to the 'Duty of Care' regulations in the Environmental Protection Act 1990, to provide training for waste management professionals who now have to satisfy the criteria of being technically competent to run waste disposal sites. Until the act was passed anyone could run a landfill site, now site managers must prove that they are fit and proper so to do.[2]

These initiatives form the background against which these guidelines have been produced. The aim is to provide examples of current good practice in areas relating to the built environment from FHE institutions, employers, professional bodies and others who are leading their fields in the promotion of the environmental agenda.[3] This document forms one of a series coordinated by the Council for Environmental Education.

1.2   The Built Environment

The 'built environment' encompasses not only individual buildings but also their surroundings and the way they come together to form villages, towns and cities. It implies not only how buildings are planned and constructed but also the materials and energy they use and their ability to be recycled or reused in whole or in part.

The built environment also cannot be separated from the communities and individuals which live and work in buildings and the effect that buildings have upon them in terms of health, safety, security, comfort and aesthetics: 'Sustainable urban development must aim to produce a city that is "user-friendly" and resourceful, in terms not only of its form and its energy efficiency but also its function, as a place for living.'[4]

Many different courses can be included in the built environment but it is impossible to draw an absolute boundary around the areas which could be considered to fall within this title. The following major disciplines may be included:

• architecture;

• building surveying;

- construction/building studies;

- quantity surveying;

- estates management;

- building services engineering;

- town planning;

- landscape architecture;

- housing;

- civil engineering.

* *Economic Significance*

The importance of the built environment in both environmental and economic terms is enormous.

The construction industry alone creates between 6 and 10 per cent of Gross Domestic Product (depending on the state of the economy) and the Energy Efficiency Office estimates that the total building stock accounts for about £21bn of the UK energy market annually and for the release to the atmosphere of some 300 million tonnes of carbon dioxide (this is, 50 per cent of the UK total).[5] From materials extraction to demolition, through the planning of our urban areas and effects on the health and well-being of a population which spends 75 per cent of its time in buildings, the potential impacts of buildings and their surroundings cannot be ignored.[6]

Environmental Impacts

The task facing FHE teachers is to communicate the environmental impacts of buildings and building materials before, during and after construction. The different effects must be weighed against the cost of adopting alternative practices. Above all students need to be aware of the choices available.

The following section describes some of the possible impacts and alternatives. The list is not intended to be definitive but rather to provide an outline of the kind of issues which could be integrated into various courses.

Impacts of energy production and use: Energy production and use has major impacts upon the environment both in terms of the depletion of non-renewable resources and in its associated potential for pollution in two main areas:

i. **The greenhouse effect**: this is the phenomenon whereby trace gases in the atmosphere absorb infra-red radiation emitted by the earth's surface, leading to a warming effect on the atmosphere. The main greenhouse gases are carbon dioxide (CO_2) – from the burning of fossil fuels, chlorofluorocarbons (CFCs) – used as insulants and refrigerants; methane – mostly from agriculture; and nitrous oxide – mainly from motor transport. Of these, CO_2 is by far the greatest contributor. Buildings are responsible for 50 per cent of all UK carbon dioxide emissions

ii. **Acid rain**: fossil fuel burning power stations are responsible for 72 per cent of all sulphur dioxide (SO_2) emissions, which along with other acid constituents fall as acid rain, causing deterioration of buildings, damage to forests and loss of life in lakes and rivers.

The question of the relationship between transport and other built environment energy uses is complex. It impinges on both road planning/construction and general town and country planning and is considered further in the section on the use of planning to avoid pollution

Energy efficiency and conservation: The efficient use and conservation of energy should form part of all built environment courses. The following areas could be considered:

•   insulation and draught-proofing;

•   Building Energy Management Systems (BEMS) and other automatic controls;

•   use of monitoring and target setting/energy auditing;

•   modelling of lighting, thermal and climatic conditions;

•   'switch-off' and 'good-housekeeping' campaigns and general energy awareness;

•   developments in low-energy appliances and clean technology;

- combined heat and power systems;

- renewable energy sources;

- low energy design and planning for energy efficiency;

- economic incentives (cost-savings/energy taxes).

Materials impacts: The choice of raw materials can greatly affect the environmental impacts of buildings for example, the production of aggregates (crushed rock, sand and gravel) is estimated to have involved land-take exceeding 2,000 ha per year since 1987.[7] This does not include land-take from stone and brick production. Recycling of materials and planning to avoid the need for road building could be discussed as mitigating measures.

Transportation impacts add another dimension to the total environmental costs of aggregates. Transportation occurs between quarries and building sites and materials are imported (and therefore transported) from abroad, at an estimated direct cost of £12m per year. This in turn adds further indirect costs in pollution from exhaust fumes, particularly CO_2 the major greenhouse gas.

Paints, solvents and timber treatments pose both direct risks to health and the risk of environmental damage during their production, use and final disposal. Borax, a non-toxic mineral, can be used in dry areas to suppress mould growth and insect attack. It also acts as a fire retardant, giving off CO_2 when heated.[8]

The construction industry has been a major user of ozone-depleting CFCs for refrigeration, air-conditioning, insulation and fire-protection materials. Many architects and developers are already specifying alternative products. Of these, HCFCs are considered to be only marginally less damaging than CFCs themselves.

Finally, deforestation contributes three to nine billion tonnes carbon dioxide each year to total CO_2 emissions. Britain is the largest importer of tropical hardwoods in Europe. In 1988 it was estimated that 50 per cent of tropical hardwood imported into Britain was used by the construction industry. Students should be warned to be wary of claims that timber comes from sustainably managed forests and should be encouraged to look for alternatives, such as temperate hard and softwoods or, preferably, using recycled timber. Larch, oak and sweet chestnut are good durable species for external wood constructions.[9]

Courses could consider the following with regard to materials:

- sources of raw materials and environmental impacts associated with extraction and transport to the point of use;

- environmental effects arising from the processing of raw materials into useful secondary materials, for example treatment of timber or manufacture of CFCs;

- environmental effects of materials in use, for example formaldehyde release from glues used with chipboard;

- environmental effects of materials in disposal/decay and the potential for reuse/recycling of materials;

- labelling of materials to provide information about their environmental effects to customers; use of life-cycle analysis to determine the total impact of a material or process over its lifetime.

Site planning impacts: Good site planning can create a healthier and more pleasing environment. The effects of bad planning are somewhat subjective and therefore harder to evaluate and need to be seen in a social as well as environmental context. All built environment students should have an understanding of how site features relate to other matters and courses could raise awareness of the following:

- existing landscape features; the ecological and archaeological importance of the site;

- the need to undertake an environmental impact assessment;

- the need to determine previous uses of the site and remediate any contamination which may have occurred. This will require careful consideration of the cost/future liability implications for all parties concerned;

- the provision of safe storage areas for products and waste on the construction site and proper arrangements for the disposal of wastes;

- impacts of the construction process, such as increased traffic volume, dust and noise.

Case Study: Legislation Case Study – Environmental Impact Assessment (EIA)

Introduced by an EC Directive in 1988, this is a technique for evaluating the environmental effects of a new development before it is allowed to proceed. Data is submitted to the Planning Authority concerning the environmental effects of the proposed development. In some cases formal environmental assessment is mandatory. In other cases, EIA is only required where there is a likelihood of significant environmental impact arising from the development.

Research by Tim Coles of the Institution of Environmental Assessment has found that the application of the Town and Country Planning (Assessment of Environmental Effects) 1988 legislation has been very patchy.[10] Two years after the introduction of the regulations 69 per cent of local authorities had not received an environmental statement.

Local authorities are permitted to adjudicate whether or not EIA is required and investigations revealed that of 24 authorities who had not received an environmental statement, 50 per cent had nevertheless had developments above the threshold of significance indicated in government guidance. The main reason given for not having requested an EIA was lack of familiarity with the regulations.

At a recent conference on environmental assessment, Dr S. Halls outlined a conceptual approach based on Integral Environmental Planning (IEP).

This would involve a 'quantified mapping of the environmental quality and environmental risks around industrial sites, and the establishment of a relationship between the various sources of emissions/risk and the environmental quality itself.' IEP has the following objectives:

• to develop industrial zones that minimise environmental impacts and risks;

• to allow the development of land for non-industrial purposes in areas where the environmental quality and quality of life for humans would be high;

• to stimulate the location of polluting industries in areas where their environmental impacts can be monitored and managed;

• to encourage planners and governments to adopt proactive environmental and decision making policies, so as to provide the foundation for sustainable development of industry based economies.[11]

Further information on planning to minimise pollution can be found in Christopher Wood's book *Planning Pollution Prevention – Anticipatory Controls over Air Pollution Sources*.[12]

It has also been suggested that changes are required to the law to reduce conflict and overlap between the environmental assessment regulations and the authorisation process for Integrated Pollution Control (IPC) under the Environmental Protection Act (1990). Companies must currently apply for authorisation from Her Majesty's Inspectorate of Pollution (HMIP) if they intend to carry out certain proscribed processes.

This can lead to developers having to supply two separate assessments – one to the planning authority and the second to HMIP. A recent report has shown that there are many areas of overlap between the processes subject to each regime. However the requirements of the two authorities may be in conflict, for example, a planning authority may require a company to build short stack to minimise visual intrusion, whereas HMIP would recommend a higher stack to allow adequate dispersion of pollutants.[13]

Legislation is under constant revision in these kinds of areas and both FHE teachers and professional bodies require continual updating to keep pace. The need for cooperation between clients, designers and builders should be stressed. In product specification all noxious substances must be assessed under the Control of Substances Hazardous to Health (COSHH) regulations and their use diminished or eliminated, so as to prevent unnecessary risks to the health and well-being of construction workers.

Building design: This will affect the environmental impact of the building over its entire lifetime. The following could be considered:

- the need to create an aesthetically pleasing, accessible and safe environment for all potential users of the development;

- energy efficiency measures;

- water conservation measures;

- materials used (see above);

- provision of recycling and waste disposal facilities;

- the need to provide a healthy internal environment;

- designing for durability and allowing internal adaptation to meet changing needs;

- the conservation of existing buildings and the importance of building reuse, as well as new build.

In the commercial and industrial sectors, there is a preference for constructing new buildings rather than rehabilitating existing structures.[14] However, a number of projects have converted abandoned industrial premises, creating multi-use work spaces for small firms or even residential blocks in former factory/warehouse sites. Discussion should be encouraged around the potential cost and environmental issues involved in both new build and reuse of buildings. Methods for upgrading existing buildings and the ethics and economics of adaptation and reuse could also be considered.

Pollution and Hazardous Substances: The pollution of the urban environment arises from a number of sources – some may be easily traceable, such as dark smoke from a chimney stack, but for most gradual pollution, including contamination of land and groundwater, it is difficult to determine the exact origin or extent of the effects. This means that all those who purchase land now have to be vigilant to avoid buying an area which may be contaminated and for which the purchaser may become liable for clean-up costs.

Companies in all sectors, including construction and development, are also increasingly wary of creating sudden, unintentional releases of pollutants. These can give rise to bad publicity and loss of faith by the general public. Pollution arising from transport is also an area of significant concern. Courses could examine the following:

- regulations governing the release of pollutants;

- types of pollutant – effects on air, water, soil, fauna, flora, and human health;

- reducing pollution through clean technology, materials or product substitution;

- liability issues;

- the 'polluter pays' principle;

- industrial hazards and risk assessments.

1.3   Students are the Professionals of the Future

The pressure on industry to operate within an environmentally conscious framework reflects the growing awareness and concern of the general public with regard to environmental issues. It is to be expected that today's students will take with them into industry a well-developed sense of environmental responsibility and that those already in the workplace respond to conscience as well as market forces and legislation in wanting to adopt greener practices.

The guidelines and case studies in this booklet can only provide a basic checklist of the material which could be included in built environment courses. Attention has been paid to both the required environmental content and the methodology for incorporating the material into existing courses. In summary, built environment courses should include the following areas at a depth relevant to the overall nature of the course:

- economic and social impacts of the built environment;

- impacts associated with energy production and use;

- renewable sources of energy:

- energy efficiency and energy conservation;

- impacts of different materials;

- alternative materials, eco-labelling and life-cycle analysis;

- waste disposal, reuse and recycling;

- site planning and environmental assessment;

- land use and conservation of land;

- building conservation, adaptation, reuse;

- pollution – hazards and liabilities;

- the internal environment – sick building syndrome/thermal comfort.

Case Study: Planning and Sustainable Development, University of the West of England (Faculty of the Built Environment in the School of Town and Country Planning)

It is now possible to define two major strands in planning for environmental quality. One is concerned with the aesthetic response to the environment: the feel, touch, look, smell and taste of the environment; its associations, convenience, beauty and liveability. The other is concerned with the sustainability of the environment, its ability to support the human species: its basic resources of earth, air, climate, water, energy and diversity of life forms. These two strands interact in quite profound ways.

The prime aim of the course is to explore the term sustainable development and how we might try to plan to achieve it. This exploration will take energy as a key theme: the generation and use of energy in the Built Environment; the implications for pollution and the natural environment.

A second aim is to examine the degree to which planning for sustainable development is consistent with other planning goals, and particularly with design for high aesthetic quality. In terms of style, the aim is to learn as much as possible by actually *doing*. The heart of the course (and a major slice of the assessment) is therefore a project. The purpose of the project is also to develop spatial planning skills and sensitivity. The hope is to develop a course which achieves high quality and specialist knowledge, helping to set the planning agenda for the next decade.

Seminar 1: Urban Design for Sustainability

What might be a design brief for sustainable development? Aspects include: local energy supply/district heating; energy efficient design; solar layout; microclimate; landscape and planting; density patterns; wastes, sewage, recycling; local pedestrian accessibility; localised facilities. The focus is a three dimensional design.

Seminar 2: Sustainable Urban Form

What broad urban forms are the most sustainable? Aspects include: public transport; car restraint; park and ride; housing location, commercial location; densities; energy supply; pollution adsorption; wildlife; urban containment.

Seminar 3: Sustainable Energy Strategies

What could be a rational and sustainable UK energy strategy? Aspects include: non-renewable and renewable energy resources; pollution from fossil fuels; the nuclear issue; the potential for energy-efficiency; domestic, industrial, commercial and transport sectors; privatisation; the energy supply industries.

Case Study: Third year Architecture Project at the University of Bath

The object of this project was to prepare a detailed design for a retreat, commissioned by the Gaia Trust, to be built in a remote area. In addition to submitting their designs, students were asked to imagine how the future occupants would utilise the building and submit an instruction manual to illustrate this. No mains services were allowed and the retreat had to be designed according to low energy principles.

The students were told the facilities should comprise:

- parking space for at least three cars or transit vans;

- sleeping places for at least 13 people, of whom three may be assumed to be infants;

- toilet and washing facilities;

- a place to cook and serve meals for all the occupants together;

- a place to relax or play;

- a place to study;

- a place outdoors to eat meals, relax, play or study.

The major constraints that had to be considered by the students included the following:

- no mains gas;

- no mains electricity;

- no mains water;

- no mains sewerage;

- no refuse collection;

- low CO_2 in production;

- low CO_2 in use.

2   ENVIRONMENTAL EDUCATION RELATING TO THE DEVELOPMENT OF PERSONAL VALUES, ATTITUDES AND ACTIONS

Further and Higher Education institutions are potential 'multipliers' in terms of promoting sustainable practice, because of the rapid turnover of students and because today's students are often tomorrow's influential decision-makers. (Shirley Ali Khan, 1991)

Students need to develop a sense of personal environmental responsibility and an understanding of how their own lifestyles impact on the environment. Courses need to be designed to stress the implications of individual actions and may be illustrated with reference to:

- links between the lifestyle of developed countries and global resource depletion and the need to alter current behaviour;

- future impacts if similar levels of consumption are reached in developing countries as they are in developed countries, and the need to provide appropriate technological assistance and a more equitable system of trade and resource distribution;

- socio-economic issues, such as poverty, population growth, migration and war, which impact heavily on the environment;

- basic scientific principles for modelling climate change and eco-system disturbance, and the problems associated with verification of varied causes and effects;

- the recognition that our interactions with nature are not merely utilitarian but have aesthetic and spiritual aspects;

- the meaning of sustainable development and the options open to individuals, groups and organisations (including industry and commerce) for its achievement.

2.1   Relating Global Concepts to Individual Lifestyles

To bring these wide-reaching concepts into a manageable framework, simple connections need to be made highlighting the power of individuals as consumers of products and energy, producers of waste, and participants in local and national decision-making.

The student, like the industrialist, needs to be able to make critical choices, particularly where short-term financial gain and long-term ecological sustainability fall into conflict. There is only a matter of scale between a student choosing to purchase a low energy lamp and an energy manager switching an entire workplace to low energy lighting.

Given that many organisations still demand a simple payback period of three years or less on investments in energy-conserving or clean-technology, there is still enormous ground to cover in persuading the commercial world to consider the implications of their current activities for future generations.

FHE institutions generally have multi-million pound turn-overs and extensive estates, consume large amounts of water, energy, paper and other materials, and are producers of waste, including hazardous and clinical wastes (albeit in tiny quantities compared to industry). They are also served by various modes of transport and provide catering facilities for staff and students. The range of environmental impacts is therefore very large.[15] Their ability to influence staff and student behaviour is correspondingly great.

Development of an environmental strategy can benefit a higher education institution by:

- reducing costs through energy efficiency and waste reduction;

- improving recruitment potential on the basis of having a proven record of environmental good practice;

- improving communication within and between departments;

- improving campus appearance and working conditions.

Within schools of the built environment, there is ample opportunity to use the institutions' own building stock as the basis for project work. Liaison between teaching staff in built environment faculties and university estates managers should be encouraged. Building and estates departments are useful sources of information on the problems of dealing with real buildings. Equally students can provide a valuable resource in monitoring and auditing conditions on campus. However, communication between support staff and academics has often been minimal or even hostile, leading to lost opportunities for valuable collaboration.

An institution itself dedicated to good environmental practice will have far greater credibility in teaching students the importance of environmental responsibility. Institutions may well derive a market advantage by attracting students on the basis of such a reputation.

Case Study: Institutional Greening as an Educational Resource, Anglia Polytechnic University

Anglia Polytechnic University is a multi-campus regional university. To cope with planned growth in student numbers, it is constructing a new campus in Chelmsford to replace existing accommodation (40,000m^2 of accommodation on a site of about 9 ha, previously used for industrial purposes close to the city centre). The university is committed to developing an energy efficient, environmentally conscious building design.

A building's energy analysis is not regarded as a secondary exercise to improve the initial design, or to comply with building regulations, but as central in the design thinking. A comprehensive energy masterplan, based on the performance concept of design, is being established for the whole campus.

The university energy policy aims to:

- minimise CO_2 emission related to the construction and operation of the new buildings;

- help reduce ozone-depletion by eliminating the use of CFCs;

- minimise energy-related running costs;

- minimise the maintenance burden of the campus;

- provide low energy buildings at little or no extra cost.

This policy is being realised by:

- providing low energy guidance notes for the design of each building type;

- the use of simulation techniques, using the performance concept of design, regarding the ventilation, heating, cooling and lighting requirements of each building;

- maximising passive environmental design, reducing the active building services requirements. The passive environmental design strategy not only promotes low energy design but encourages simple durable low maintenance systems;

- provision of self-contained energy blocks permitting the idea of assessment of the separate energy needs of each building type;

- exploitation of the natural features of the site to maximise passive solar energy and use thermal storage systems for both heating and cooling;

- providing very high standards of thermal insulation where high occupancy patterns for long periods will realise large energy savings;

- follow-up monitoring of energy consumption to help realise the potential energy saving.

The new campus will offer the opportunity to use the design, construction and management of the total complex for teaching and research activities in the fields of energy, construction and facilities management. Consideration is being given to the inclusion of these opportunities in undergraduate studies. Further monitoring of performance may also provide a basis for higher degrees and research. Dissemination of energy/green training will also be possible through seminars and other media.

Case Study: Collaboration between Building and Estates Department and the School of the Built Environment, De Montfort University

At De Montfort University, Leicester, students have used the campus buildings for many years for project work but the information gathered has never previously been used by the institution for its own purposes. Now, as one of the initiatives stemming from a new energy policy, the Building and Estates Department plans to draw up a list of building monitoring projects which would be suitable for student involvement.[16]
   A new school of Engineering and Manufacture has recently been constructed, which is the largest passively ventilated building in Europe. The performance of this building will be monitored, using students and specialists. In addition, all the students attending classes in the building are aware of its low energy design. It therefore acts as an awareness-raising vehicle in itself.

Promotion of environmental good practice on campus should encourage staff and students to adopt similar behaviour in their personal lives. Simple, transferable measures include:

- energy efficiency measures, turning off unnecessary appliances (especially lights), insulation and draught-proofing, purchasing low energy appliances and keeping doors and windows closed;

- water conservation measures, turning off dripping taps, installing spray taps and controlled flush WCs;

- reducing waste, recycling or reusing materials when possible;

- opting for public transport, car-sharing, biking or walking;

- using consumer power, buying locally-produced, recycled, organic, fair-trade or eco-labelled products.

These personal gestures can be linked in teaching to the much more dramatic effects of business making similar choices. Energy and waste management have been prioritised by many of the larger companies, whilst the field of trying to determine the true environmental impact of products, processes and systems is ever-growing through the discipline of life-cycle assessment. Green economics and full-cost pricing, the growth in environmental legislation and the use of fiscal instruments (such as the proposed carbon tax) are new elements which need to be integrated into the curriculum if students are to be fully competent to deal with life in the business world of the future.

Case Study: Design & Ecology course 1992, University of Central England

This course uses a variety of means to develop both personal and business-related awareness of the environment, including visits to relevant exhibitions and a trip to the Centre for Alternative Technology at Machynlleth.

The course consists of eight sessions divided into lectures and seminars with site visits to exhibitions in Birmingham and Wales.

1st Week:

Lecture: **Introduction to ecological design and the industrial society**

The roots of ecological design in the nineteenth and twentieth centuries; modern design and ecology; critics of the industrial society from Mumford to Illich.

Discussion: What is ecological design?

Seminar: Students choose seminar and essay topics

2nd Week:

Lecture: **Ecological Design: Resources and Energy**
Main environmental issues and their implications for design; proposals for long- and short-term changes.

Seminar: Visit to the ECODESIGN exhibition in Perry Barr

3rd Week:

Lecture: **Intermediate Technology: Schumacher and his Influence**
The writing of E.F. Schumacher and its implications for design; the Intermediate Technology group and design in the Third World; the Schumacher Society.

Seminar: Tutorials

4th Week:

Lecture: **The Green movement in the 1970s and 1980s**
Friends of the Earth and Greenpeace; the self-sufficiency movement in the 1970s; the New Age; the Centre for Alternative Technology; Women's Environmental Network.

Seminar:*   Ecological Architecture and design in the 1970s. Victor Papanek; ICSID 'Design for Need', 1976; Radical Technology: The Autonomous House; garbage Housing

5th Week:

Lecture: **Media, Business and Green Economics**
Sustainability; the New Consumer; alternative trading; Traidcraft; green capitalism; environmental audits; New Economics Foundation.

Seminar:*   Green Consumerism: for and against; advertising and marketing of Green products – FOE Green 'Con' awards.

Visit: Green Show at the NEC

6th Week:

Lecture: **Graphic Design and Ecology: introduction**
Seminar:*   Recycled paper, packaging, eco-labelling, green logos, animation and TV graphics; Michael Peters; Bodyshop.

Visit: Machynlleth, Centre for Alternative Technology

7th Week:
Lecture: **Product Design and the Environment: introduction**
Seminar:* Design for re-use, repair, re-manufacture, recycling; transport;
            equipment; furniture; green design and the craft revival

8th Week:
Lecture: **Ecological Architecture: introduction**
Seminars:* Sick Building Syndrome; Building Biology; the green office;
            the green home; self-build; solar villages
*= student seminars

Students are required to produce one piece of work for this course, either
a seminar paper or an essay equivalent to 3,000 words. Topics may be
chosen from the above list or the student may suggest his/her own, after
checking with the tutor.

2.2   Linking Personal Choices to Built Environment Teaching

The sustainable management of resources through energy conservation
and waste reduction is increasingly perceived as good business practice,
not simply good environmental practice. In built environment courses the
following may be highlighted:

- energy efficiency, target setting and monitoring;

- low energy design;

- waste reduction, reuse and recycling of materials;

- sources and types of raw materials – renewable/non-renewable;

- transport issues;

- building conservation/refurbishment versus new build;

- water resources – effects of construction/operation of buildings on water
  table;

- pollution of air, water, soil;

- climatic effects;

- developments in clean technology;

- land use issues/conservation;

- green economics and the evaluation of the total cost of environmental degradation;

- environmental legislation, fiscal and policy measures;

- environmental liability;

- contaminated land issues;

- green design and green marketing;

- the interaction between environmental issues and social issues.

Case Study: BTEC Learning Outcomes for Environmental Responsibility[17]

On completion of the unit the learner should be able to:

- explain the principles of sustainability;

- justify her/his own environmental values and attitudes;

- appreciate, in general terms, global and local environmental interconnections;

- recognise the environmental implications of his/her personal behaviour;

- make personal decisions which take account of the environment.

2.3   The Existing Penetration of Environmental Teaching

The teaching of Energy and the Environment is not treated with urgency – given the scale of the problems which society as a whole is confronting.[18]

In a 1988 survey of attitudes of heads of schools of architecture and specialist energy lecturers, over 75 per cent gave support to the idea that energy efficiency was 'very important at undergraduate and postgraduate level.' However, this perception did not seem to be reflected in the actual level of teaching of energy-related topics.[19] Similarly, teachers generally reported a belief that the earth's climate is changing as a result of global warming but this was not found to be integrated into studio work undertaken by architecture students. Where there is an appreciable environmental content, this is often the work of individual enthusiasts involved in course design and not a departmental or institutional policy decision.

Susan Roaf in her 1991 survey found that schools do teach enough about heat, light and sound to equip students to cope with the requirements of building performance, at least up to current building regulations standards. However, at least some of the teachers taking on environmental issues in the classroom felt that they were marginalised from the main stream of teaching. It was also noted that the environmental course content may be taught by different staff to those supervising studio work, leading to a lack of integration. Other problems highlighted by Dr Roaf included a general lack of communication between schools on course content and form and a lack of funds to buy hardware, software and specialist teaching for energy and environmental auditing programmes.[20]

Dr Roaf's research was only concerned with schools of architecture but similar problems would seem to apply across other Built Environment curricula.

In gathering material for this report, many establishments' initial response indicated some confusion as to what really constitutes environmental education. It was generally felt that all Built Environment courses automatically cover environmental themes making it impossible to separate the environmental element from the course as a whole. However, examples cited often lacked the holistic approach to environmental teaching that is required if true cross-curricular greening is to be achieved. For example, although courses in Urban Renewal would be expected to cover issues such as the use of derelict land, which is undoubtedly environmental, there is no indication that such issues are placed in the global environmental context.

3   ENVIRONMENTAL EDUCATION FOR BUSINESS AND PROFESSIONAL VALUES

Sadly, due to a dominant economic paradigm taught in our institutions of learning world-wide, we are suffering from the ever increasing degradation of the environment. Fortunately, no consciously competent professor of economics would perpetuate this myth in their teaching in the 1990s. There has been an awakening as to the value and scarcity of natural resources. Hence the new term in economist jargon 'Full cost pricing', which will have an astounding impact on business and economics in the future. (Gary Owen, 1992)[21]

3.1   The Need for Corporate Environmentalism

The dominant economic paradigm described above has long created a separation between personal values held by some individuals and groups, promoting conservation and environmentally responsible behaviour, and business values, which have been oriented towards making profit whatever the environmental cost. However, the current level of environmental degradation and consequent public outcry is now so great that companies are being forced to examine the total cost of their activities – that is, the direct and indirect costs plus the costs of the environmental damage caused.

For example, a forest clearance would involve not only the costs of labour, machinery, transport and so on but also the loss of productivity of the soil, erosion, pollution of groundwaters and water-table effects, social effects on forest-dwellers and so on; each of these impacts creating its own financial burden. This extra cost has normally been borne by the poorest members of global society, since they are the most likely to live in polluted areas, to farm the most marginal lands and carry out work, such as mining, which carries risks to health. In the so-called third world, large development projects have expelled entire communities from their lands and destroyed the ecosystems on which they depend, whilst failing to provide them with a sustainable alternative lifestyle.

The effects of this unbridled push to develop are now being felt in Western industrialised nations in the form of lost biodiversity, global climate change and threats to national security and increased relative and absolute poverty. The result is a growing recognition of the need to implement environmental strategy at corporate level, for the polluter to bear the cost of pollution and for each individual to be aware of their own responsibility for environmental protection in the workplace.

3.2   Environmental Pressures on Business

Market forces and increased national, European and international legislation are bringing pressure to bear on the professions to move towards a form of economic growth which can satisfy the needs of the present generation without jeopardising the needs of future generations.[22] This so-called sustainable development can only be achieved with due regard to the way in which we utilise the earth's resources. Awareness of the need to conserve scarce resources, such as fossil fuels and, in many places, water, is being matched by an awareness of the need to preserve sites of archaeological and cultural importance and areas of natural beauty and wilderness.

Consequently, the business sector is now subject to a number of sources of pressure to mitigate its impact on the environment, which can be grouped as follows:-

•   legislation;

•   fiscal and policy measures;

•   market pressures;

•   pressure from environmental activists and the public.

Legislation

The amount of legislation to which companies are subjected is everincreasing. In the UK much of the statute is derived from European Community directives, which are then established in our own law by acts of parliament or statutory instruments. International agreements, such as the Montreal Protocol (on the phased elimination of CFC production) also influence government policy and statute.

It is outside the scope of this document to examine the wealth of legislation relevant to environmental control in the UK. However, a number of guiding principles run through much of the recently introduced statutes:

•   **The polluter pays' principle**: this states that as far as possible, those responsible for creating environmental pollution should bear the financial burden of cleaning up. This is best seen in the issuing of consents for discharge of effluent to water and authorisations for emissions to air, for which companies are charged by the regulatory authorities.

However, where no single company or site can be identified as the source of a pollutant, identifying who should be responsible and how much they should be expected to pay can become decidedly complex. This may be the case where several similar companies release effluent to the same water course or in the case of surface water run-off, where a number of sites have contributed to the contamination.

- **The 'precautionary' principle**: this states that because environmental effects are often complex, science and technology cannot always give exact answers as to the extent and nature of environmental degradation from a particular action or contaminant. It is therefore wise and prudent to assume that damage is being caused and to act to remedy this, wherever there is some evidence to suggest this is happening – even if this does not constitute proof.

  For example, there is continuing debate as to whether the earth is now undergoing a gradual process of warming due to the build up of gases, such as carbon dioxide and methane, in the atmosphere. Different models give different predictions of the consequences of global warming. Nevertheless, the UK government has made a commitment to reduce the levels of carbon dioxide being released back to 1990 levels by the year 2000.

- **Integrated pollution control**: prior to the passing of the 1990 Environmental Protection Act, pollution of air, water and soil were regulated by different authorities and were treated as essentially different issues. The 1990 act has implemented an integrated approach to pollution control, at least for the most toxic (so-called 'red list') substances. It has been proposed that eventually all pollution control will be fully integrated and regulated by a single Environmental Protection Agency. It is likely to take quite some time before such a fully integrated system is realised, as the historical differences in practice and expertise of the different regulatory bodies (local authorities, Her Majesty's Inspectorate of Pollution and the National Rivers Authority) are not easy to marry together.

- **BATNEEC (Best Available Techniques Not Entailing Excessive Cost)**: an EC-derived term, now incorporated into the Environmental Protection Act. When a company applies for authorization to carry out its processes, it must demonstrate to the regulatory authority that BATNEEC is being applied to protect the environment from harm.

Companies are expected to use the most effective technology and management processes available to safeguard the environment, providing that adopting such measures will not threaten their commercial viability.

• **BPEO (Best Practicable Environmental Option)**: under Integrated Pollution Control (IPC), where a company has a choice of disposal route for a waste or contaminant, they must chose the route that is least environmentally harmful, providing this is technically and economically possible.

• **Duty of care**: all those involved with the disposal of wastes have an obligation to ensure that disposal takes place with due regard to environmental consequences. This was also introduced in the Environmental Protection Act 1990. In particular, anyone operating a landfill site must be able to demonstrate that they are competent and that adequate measures are being taken to deal with methane generation and leachate within the site.

• **Sustainable development**: at the time of writing, March 1994, no statute had as yet been passed which is directly related to sustainable development as proposed in Agenda 21. However, a range of statutory, fiscal and policy measures will need to be used if this is to become a viable aim.

Fiscal and Policy Measures

These include preferential taxation measures and creating tradeable permits for pollution. The UK government announced in the 1992 White Paper on the Environment that it favoured the use of economic instruments to regulation as a pollution control measure. The most famous of these is the proposed EC carbon/energy tax, which has been under consideration for a number of years but has so far failed to materialise. Instead the government has recently introduced VAT on domestic fuel use.

The government released a guide to the use of economic instruments in 1993. 'Tradeable permits' works on the basis that where a company is emitting less of a given substance than it is permitted to, it may sell off its remaining authorised capacity to another company, which is emitting more than its permitted level. It is likely that such a system will be introduced for sulphur dioxide emissions in the first instance. It remains to be seen how well this will protect sensitive areas from increased acidification.[23]

Market Forces

Legislation is not the only driving force behind businesses changing their attitudes towards the environment. The costs associated with pollution incidents or other environmental damage can extend beyond the fear of prosecution. Typically, costs may arise through:

- loss of public support – particularly where wildlife or communities are harmed by a pollution incident;

- loss of production;

- site remediation costs;

- costs of implementing reactive measures to prevent reoccurrence of the pollution incident (often more expensive than precautionary measures introduced through strategic planning);

- cost of monitoring long-term effects of the incident;

- cost of dealing with liability/damages claims.

Environmental and community groups have also been placing pressure on industry to behave in an environmentally responsive fashion. Opposition to the planned £23bn roads expansion programme has been particularly vociferous but out-of-town shopping malls and other developments have also become scenes of confrontation between developers and protestors in recent years.

Professional campaigning groups, such as Friends of the Earth and Greenpeace, are now regularly called upon to advise government select committees, as they are responsible for much of the independent research carried out into environmental effects.

Customers and suppliers may also exert pressure on a company to adopt an environmental policy. For example, four of the big DIY stores, including B&Q and Texas, are refusing to stock any timber which is not certified as being obtained from a sustainably managed source as from 1995. The pressure of market forces can be clearly seen in the push towards the eco-labelling of products and the formulation of accreditation schemes for environmental management systems (EMS), such as the new British Standard 7750.

SABA.

3.3   Responses to Environmental Pressures

Larger companies in high impact industries, such as petrochemicals and paper and packaging, have for some time used environmental auditing as a management tool for reducing their negative impacts on the environment. This is a voluntary process undergone in response to both marketplace pressures and the need to comply with environmental legislation.

Environmental audit is defined as a management tool which comprises a systematic, documented, periodic and objective evaluation of how well the organisation, management and equipment is performing with the aim of helping to safeguard the environment by: facilitating management control of environmental practices; assessing compliance with company policies, which would include the need to meet any regulatory requirements. Companies undergoing environmental audits make a commitment at senior management level to improve their environmental performance and set up an environmental policy outlining their objectives. Performance is then monitored. The results of the monitoring are audited at intervals to ensure that targets are being met and to allow the updating of the policy.

The construction industry is the only high impact industry where a significant number of large operators have not used environmental audits.

Environmental audits are one management tool available to companies. If they wish to go a step further they may set an Environmental Management System (EMS). This is simply an organisational structure, detailing the responsibilities, procedures, processes and resources to be used for environmental management. A number of such systems are being developed which will allow companies to receive an accreditation certificate for their EMS. The most well known of these is the British Standard 7750. A second system called the Environmental Management and Eco-Audit Scheme is being developed in the European Community.

Environmental Management Systems – BS 7750
Following the success of the earlier BS 5750 in persuading companies to adopt a quality management system, BS 7750 requires that a company adopt a similar management system to control its impacts on the environment.

Case Study: The Construction Industry Training Board (One-day course in Environmental Management in Construction/BS 7750)

This one-day course is designed to help those already in the construction industry to carry out an environmental review of their company, how to react to current legislation and how to develop an environmental policy. By the end of the course delegates should be able to:

- list the key areas of environmental concern;

- list construction specific areas;

- explain the benefits to be gained from environmental management;

- understand BS 7750 and its relationship with other standards;

- develop an environmental policy for their company;

- raise awareness within their company about the policy and individual roles;

- plan the development of their own Environmental Management System;

- appreciate the need for environmental assessment.

The course is aimed at middle to senior management, particularly those responsible for strategic decision-making and resource allocation.

Case Study: Bovis Construction Limited, Environmental Policy

The environmental policy of Bovis Construction Limited has been included here as a typical example of a company environmental policy. It contains no specific targets but outlines a basic set of principles for environmental awareness and care.

BOVIS CONSTRUCTION LIMITED
Environmental Policy

1. Bovis Construction Limited as a major construction company, operating within the fields of Management Contracting and Construction Management in the UK, recognise that its activities have wide-ranging environmental implications in both the long and the short term. These can potentially be either damaging or beneficial.

2. The Company will therefore pursue a policy aimed at minimising environmental damage and maximising opportunities for environmental enhancement.

3. In all of its activities, including the construction of projects and in its own administration, the Company will consider environmental impact as an important part of its decision-making processes. Bovis will aim to play a major role in setting new standards for the industry in areas such as pollution control, conservation of energy and natural resources and the preservation and enhancement of natural habitats.

4. To implement this policy, the Company will ensure that its staff are aware of the environmental implications of activities within their own areas of responsibility. Where necessary, training programmes will be implemented, or outside bodies consulted, in order to heighten staff awareness of the relevant issues.

5. On individual projects, Bovis will endeavour to give or to obtain the best advice for its clients concerning environmental aspects of the project. Where it is appropriate, we will assist in tailoring designs to suit particular environmental concerns consistent with optimum solutions in cost and time.

6. During the execution of projects Bovis will manage and organise the works in a manner which will reduce, so far as is reasonably practicable, environmental damage caused by:

    *   noise
    *   dust
    *   mud on roads or footpaths
    *   effluent arising from the works

    and will take effective precautions to protect occupiers of adjacent land or buildings and the general public from any danger, discomfort, disturbance, trespass or nuisance. Such provisions will include secure, well lit and signed hoardings, barriers or screens as necessary and a well presented clean site. Bovis will use their best endeavours to protect and maintain existing services and to minimise traffic flow and noise by logistics management and off-site fabrication.

7. In pursuance of this policy, environmental considerations will be taken into account in the selection of trade contractors and sub-contractors and when assessing the acquisition of plant and materials from trade sources.

8. All members of the Company's staff will be expected to be aware of and to pursue this policy.

C. J. Spackman
Chairman and Managing Director
Prepared in conjunction with David Bellamy Associates 1989

This is only one stage in the environmental management cycle and to ensure compliance with the policy environmental impacts need to be documented and the policy subject to regular review.

In order to acquire the standard the company must:

- make a commitment at senior management level to environmental improvement;

- carry out an initial review of all impacts;

- formulate an environmental policy;

- compile a register of all relevant environmental legislation;

- compile a register of all environmental impacts;

- set targets for improvement;

- establish a documented management structure for reaching targets;

- train staff to fulfil their environmental obligations;

- audit and document progress on reaching targets;

- submit a full environmental statement to the accrediting body;

- update the environmental policy and targets according to the audit results, so as to achieve continuous improvement in environmental performance.

At their best, EMSs will lead to continuous environmental improvement of participating companies, with knock-on effects expected in a raising of the general standard of environmental performance across the marketplace.

Potential benefits to the company arising from implementation of an EMS include:

- identification of cost-savings through energy conservation, use of cleaner technology and waste minimisation;

- identification of (and chance to remedy) any non-compliance with legislation;

- improved working conditions and raised staff awareness/morale;

- provision of evidence to customers of environmental commitment;

- improved environmental performance;

- a foundation for good relations with shareholders, investors, funding bodies and the regulatory authorities.

Fulfilment of all the criteria of the accrediting body leads to the awarding of a logo, which can then be used to promote a green image on publicity materials (but not products, which will be covered under a different scheme).

A similar accreditation scheme is being developed through the EC Directive on Eco-auditing and Environmental Management Systems. These are voluntary schemes but many companies perceive that they will become important factors for their public image and continued prosperity. In addition, trade associations and professional bodies are developing their own codes of environmental practice to which their members are expected to conform. In the case of the British Aggregate Construction Materials Industries (BACMI), the code is mandatory and obliges member companies to publish results of site audits.[24]

These codes and schemes often recommend environmental consideration to be made beyond the practice required by current statute.

Problems with BS 7750
The new British Standard was launched in 1992 and is now nearing the end of its pilot programme, and a number of problems and criticisms of the scheme are now being voiced. For example:

- the scheme is supposed to be fully compatible with the proposed European eco-audit and environmental management directive but there have been problems achieving full integration;

- companies do not have to publish the full results of their audits;

- major questions are still being raised about the required qualifications for independent certifiers – there is a lack of personnel with sufficient knowledge to judge whether companies are complying fully with the standard;[25]

- companies participating in the pilot scheme have been found to be strong on drawing up environmental policies and preliminary reviews but weak in providing training, resources and setting environmental targets;[26]

Figure 1: Outline of the BS 7750 EMS

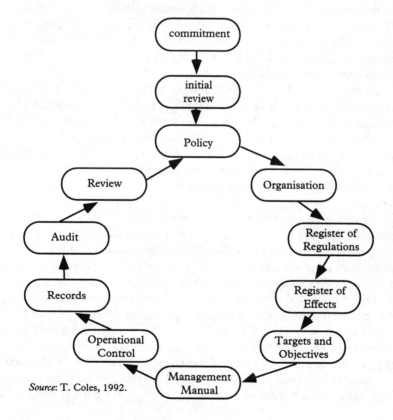

Source: T. Coles, 1992.

- take-up is expected to be high among larger firms but low among small- and medium-sized enterprises, which make up 90 per cent of British companies.

It therefore seems likely that despite a wish to appear environmentally conscious, many companies are still reluctant to cover the full cost of improvements.

Eco-labelling

EMS provides a means to reach accreditation for the entire operation of a given business or organisation. For specific household products, such as paper, washing machines and detergents, a separate system of eco-labelling is being developed in the EC.

In the built environment field, where many of the products used have a high environmental impact, a similar scheme could allow designers and developers to choose less damaging products. However, the total assessment of any product or material is an enormously complex task. Many of the environmental effects may be difficult to quantify and even quantifiable effects may be difficult to compare across different products. For example, how can the environmental damage due to dioxin release from an incinerator be compared to the global warming potential of controlled burning of methane from a landfill?

A major tool to determine the total environmental profile of a product (or process) is *Life-cycle Analysis*. This is a cradle-to-grave analysis of all the stages of a product's life from the extraction of the raw materials to its final disposal. Full LCAs are costly and time-consuming to produce and there is very rarely complete data available for all the stages. Extraction of the raw materials may take place in a different country from production and use of the product, which adds to the problems of information gathering.

Providing the 'systems boundary' (the outline of what is included and excluded from the LCA) is clearly stated, and it can allow products to be compared and can therefore assist in the establishment of criteria for eco-labels. It is important that eco-labels are seen to be independently awarded and that the criteria used are understood by both customers and suppliers of products. Eco-labelling with regard to energy efficiency is also being introduced. The National Homes Energy Rating Scheme (NHER), for example, is now firmly established as a means of determining the energy efficiency of housing stock. This is a major project run by the National Energy Foundation to encourage energy efficiency in all types of UK homes.

The NHER scheme is based on several microcomputer programmes. Each programme produces a consistent rating, on a scale of nought to ten, with ten being the most energy efficient. New homes, which meet the 1990 Building Regulations are typically rated about seven.

The rating process produces estimates of a home's running costs, and shows how these costs may be reduced by various efficiency measures. The rating is applicable to both new and existing homes and enables real comparisons to be made between homes of all ages and types. Qualified assessors issue certificates confirming the rating achieved.

Case Study: BTEC HNC Housing Studies Course: Energy Efficient and Environmentally Friendly Housing, De Montfort University, Leicester

This course aims to: develop an awareness of energy conservation and the environmental impact of house construction and refurbishment; appreciate the contribution that can be made to energy conservation and environmental protection by building environmentally sensitive and energy efficient housing; and appreciate the economic implications of energy conservation. Course objectives are as follows:

• to receive and respond to a range of information;

• to use a variety of information sources;

• to develop skills in oral presentation;

• to use a range of technological equipment (computer hardware and software);

• to produce an energy rating of an existing domestic dwelling;

• to suggest a range of practical energy saving measures to improve the energy rating obtained above.

Stage 1: Group work – Energy Awareness
Working in tutorial groups, students are required to research into selected topics relating to energy use in the UK housing stock and to possible conservation measures. This work is concluded with the submission of a written group report on an allocated topic and a short oral presentation of the group's findings. Topics are selected from the following titles:

• Energy use in UK housing: the potential for savings

- The contribution to the Greenhouse Effect made by housing in the UK and its significance

- System-built housing – energy issues with particular reference to practical conservation measures

- Nineteenth-century terraced housing – energy issues with particular reference to energy conservation measures

Stage 2: Individual work – Energy Audit
Individually students are required to carry out an energy audit of his/her own home and produce an NHER rating using the National Energy Foundation's *Home Rater* software. To complete this stage students are required to submit a full print out of the computer run of their house. This work is assessed before moving on to the next stage.

Stage 3: Evaluation of Conservation Alternatives
Using the Home Rater programme, students have to investigate some of the energy-saving options that could be applied to their own house and select those which, in their judgement, represent the most cost-effective choices. It is expected that students use their experience and research findings to consider the practicality and acceptability of their choices.

The Building Research Establishment Environmental Assessment Method (BREEAM): The Building Research Establishment has its own assessment method for examining the environmental quality of buildings at the design stage. This is called BREEAM. If assessment is carried out at the design stage it allows improvements to be made before the design is fixed.

There are BREEAM assessment questionnaires for new offices, homes and supermarkets. The scheme is voluntary and uses independent assessors to evaluate the likely impacts of the proposed building. On completion of the assessment, a certificate is issued which confirms the areas of environmental concern and criteria that the building design has satisfied.

The Building Research Establishment (BRE) also provide general information on energy efficiency in buildings and carry out research into all areas of building design and use.

Case Study: OPET Workshop – Environmental Assessment for Buildings
A course outline for a workshop on the use of BREEAM is given and other building and energy-related issues is given below. Also shown is an outline for conference held at The Building Research Establishment aimed at teachers on energy-related courses.

3.4   Conflicts and Disputes

Inevitably there will be times when both the student and the professional have to deal with conflict. Where environmental matters are concerned this may arise due to higher costs associated with environmentally responsible practice or may be associated with the different perceptions of what is valuable.

In the case of development of green-field sites, road building and the extension of industrial activities with high environmental impact, developers, construction companies and their clients are facing unprecedented opposition. For example, the recent case of the M3 extension built at Twyford Down saw unprecedented conflict between developers and protesters and called into question the usefulness of statutory protection for both ancient monuments and conservation areas (Sites of Special Scientific Interest or SSSIs). At Twyford, the conflict did not solely involve those who did not want the road battling with those who did. There were also groups who wanted to see the road built, but not by the chosen route. The European Community also became involved in this particular dispute over the question of whether the Department of Transport had complied with the EC directive on environmental impact assessment. The number of stakeholders was therefore high and the confrontation was drawn out and often violent.

In order to avoid such violent and costly disputes, the use of a technique called Alternative Dispute Resolution (ADR) has been suggested. The use of ADR is becoming increasingly common for solving multi-party disputes, in which traditional methods, such as litigation and arbitration, are considered too costly, time-consuming and/or unlikely to produce an outcome acceptable to all parties. It is particularly applicable in areas such as conflicts over the siting of new developments, where many diverse groups of people – residents, interest groups, contractors, developers, government and Local Authority – may have a stake in the outcome.

By bringing the parties in dispute together, through the intervention of a trained but neutral mediator, ADR provides the possibility that a consensus may be reached. This, of course, requires that all the stakeholders agree to participate and are prepared to try a different approach to resolving the dispute. Obviously, vested interests and imbalances of power between the disputants can limit the effectiveness of ADR. To be effective, ADR needs to begin as close as possible to the start of any development or contract, so that all participants maintain a sense of being able to influence the outcome.

A guidance note of the use of ADR is published by the National Joint Consultative Committee for Building (made up of RIBA, RICS, BEC, The Association of Consulting Engineers and the Confederation of Associations of Specialist Engineering Contractors).

3.5   Existing Penetration of Environmental Awareness among Professional Bodies

Research carried out by Michael Osborne and Kate Sankey of the University of Stirling as part of the programme 'Towards Environmental Competence in Scotland' produced a table of environmental content in courses accredited by Scottish professional bodies in built environment fields. (See Table 1.)

Twelve professional institutions were targeted, of whom nine responded. Eight of these offered (or in one case were about to offer) a professional qualification that included some environmental content. In this respect the built environment sector was found to be ahead of many, although 'even here, the professional bodies have for the most part moved very cautiously and progress has been greatest where (as with ... Town Planning) the nature of the discipline is such that environmental issues are unavoidable.'[27] The Toyne Report found similar results and also suspected that even where professional bodies required some environmental content this was often only seen in terms of 'local damage-limitation and prevention.'[28]

In England and Wales, the professional bodies were slow to respond to initial enquiries about their environmental requirements for validated courses and although some professional bodies stipulate an environmental element (notably RIBA), these do not seem to be followed up or strictly enforced.

The Royal Institute of Chartered Surveyors (RICS), for example, has no formal policy on environmental education but has skills panels, which upgrade surveyors' professional skills. Two such panels are called Construction and the Environment and Environmental Management. They also run a green business programme to promote good environmental practice. However, in the absence of a policy on education and the environment, it is not clear how effective these initiatives will be in the FHE sector as they are more aimed at the continuing professional development sector, or CPD.

Professional bodies seem unwilling to respond in the absence of clear guidance from government. Although the Toyne Report was commissioned by the Department for Education (DFE), none of its recommendations

3.6   Table 1: The Built and Designed Environment – list of Environmental Content in Accredited Courses in Scotland

Body	Qualification	Content	Amount
Royal Institute of Town Planners (RTPI)	Chartered town Planner	In accordance with RTPI Guideline	Not specified but 'considerable'
Architects and Surveyors Institute (ASI)	Licentiate, member and Fellow of ASI	Constructions and Buildings Regulations	30%
Incorporated Association of Architects and Surveyors (IAAS)	IAAS member exam Parts A & B	No discrete environmental content; integrated into other subjects.	Variable
Institute of Housing	A new professional qualification with some environmental content is about to be produced		
Institute of Building Control	Part 1 exam	Environmental Science: heat, thermal effects, sound, light, fire, climatic effects	12.5%
Landscape Institute	Associate or Fellow of the Landscape Institute (ALI), (FLI)	Ecology, resource assessment and capability, environmental assessment, landscape design, science and management	75%
Royal Incorporation of Architects in Scotland	Recognition of various undergrad programmes is delegated to RIBA	Green issues and energy effectiveness are included in many training programmes	
Chartered Institute of Building (CIB)	Member exam Part 1/2	Not specified	Small amount
Royal Institute of Chartered Surveyors (RICS)	Associate (ARICS)	Not specified	Not specified, but considerable in some courses

are mandatory. However, some changes to taught courses are being suggested at the European Parliament level. The committee on Energy, Research and Technology of the European Parliament has adopted a resolution on the use of bioclimatic construction technology for residential buildings and work premises. Article 4 of the resolution requests faculties of architecture in the universities of the European Union to introduce compulsory courses on bioclimatic architecture.[29] The resolution has now been sent to all the deans of architecture faculties in the EU, as well as to the Council and Commission, building workers' unions and the association of builders of the countries of the EU.

Case Study: Postgraduate Courses

A number of postgraduate courses exist which develop environmental themes relevant to the built environment in much greater depth than is evident in undergraduate courses. These fall between true updating, aimed primarily at those already in the workplace, and the basic cross-curricula provision it is hoped to develop.

i.   MSc in Architecture: Advanced Environmental and Energy Studies, University of East London

The aim of the course is to: allow the student to undertake advanced study in architecture topics in the area of environmental science; develop the student's intellectual and imaginative powers, problem-solving skills, ability to communicate, ability to see relationships within the subject areas learned and to perceive his/her field in a broader perspective.

The course addresses three inter-related areas: global factors; occupant health and environment; and thermal environment and energy efficiency.

ii.   MSc in Bio-climatic Architectural Design, Portsmouth University

This course aims to: enhance the scholarship, and particularly the research skills, of students of architecture, by equipping them with a range of conceptual and analytical skills which will be of relevance to the professional practice of architecture and allied professions concerned with construction and the management of the Built Environment; and provide a conversion course for students and professionals seeking competence in the fields of bio-climatic design, building design, building energy-use analysis, environmental analysis, and/or specialisms in lighting design, thermal design, and environmental protection of external spaces.

In addition the course seeks to: contribute to the personal development of students, and assist them to make useful contributions to their profession and society as a whole; and enable students to improve their employment prospects through the development of useful and relevant skills and knowledge, contact with professionals actively applying the principles taught in the course and through the attainment of an accredited qualification.

The lack of a formal policy on environmental education may stem from an unwillingness to place extra pressures on already overburdened (and under-resourced) courses. It may also arise because some disciplines regard themselves as inherently environmental. Town Planning is often cited in this way.

Whilst traditional town planning courses may focus on local environmental issues, there is no evidence to suggest that planning courses automatically give students a reasonable view of global environmental interactions or that planning courses turn out more environmentally conscious individuals than, for example, building services courses. In all disciplines, there is the need to supplement existing environmental elements with a wider environmental perspective.

In courses where a large part of the curriculum is determined by the validating body, it is vital that professional bodies take on the responsibility for determining an environmental policy for their own organisation and for ensuring that relevant environmental elements are included in all courses. A number of professional bodies are engaged in providing guidance to the FHE system and their members on environmental issues. Some examples are given below:

Case Study: The Royal Town Planning Institute – 'The Education of Planners'

> *Planning contributes to the management of change in the built and natural environment. Effective planning may take many forms, but requires knowledge about urban and regional change, the physical and natural environment and the social and economic environment, combined with understanding and skill in applying this knowledge to policy formulation, implementation and project development in complex political/institutional contexts.*[30]

This is a quote from the RTPI policy statement and general guidance for academic institutions offering initial professional education in planning. It covers the following areas: the qualities of a planner; the role of initial education; course form, length and mode; course content; and the qualities of an effective planning school. It is supplemented by two guidance notes; one on the accreditation process and one on content and performance criteria.

The guidance integrates the need for environmental awareness throughout and stresses the need for continual updating once the student has embarked on his/her professional career. In the Royal Town Planning Institute's policy statement it is noted that the performance criteria for values/attitudes components are hard to assess and should be approached with sensitivity. The following input indicators may be cited as evidence in this area:

- course statements on policy and objectives;

- course syllabi and reading lists (how and how far are the issues raised?);

- staff CVs (do the staff have particularly relevant research or experience);

- practice relationships (are these likely to assist student learning in this field);

- assessment procedures (how do they focus on this component).

These are matched with the following output indicators:

- the content of examination papers and course assignments (to assess how issues are addressed);

- performance in relevant examination papers and assignments;

- external examiners reports (noting if these refer to values in any way; to assess coverage, and level of work);

- review of assessed work (how are values manifested in review essays, research tasks, in practical reports?);

- discussions with graduating students (how would they approach issues);

- employers' comments (specifically on this question).

Royal Institute of British Architects
RIBA produce a number of documents which could be used as reference materials for course leaders, such as a checklist for designers to assist the design team and the client to determine energy effectiveness for new build.

In 1990, RIBA produced an 'Initial Statement on Global Warming and Ozone Depletion' through its Environmental and Energy Policy Committee (EEPC).[31] This is reproduced in full below.

RIBA Initial Policy Statement   *Style.*

1. The Architect's responsibility under the Charter of the RIBA and its Code of Conduct is constantly changing in the light of new information. A new dimension has been added to that responsibility with the increasing knowledge of the effect of human activity on the viability of the planet and on the health of human beings. The construction industry accounts for a significant portion of that activity.   *What about CIAT?*

2. The primary role of the EEPC is to monitor and evaluate this information and make it intelligible and available to members on a regular basis. The Committee will also disseminate decisions and recommendations produced by international bodies and research organisations concerned with combating global warming and environmental degradation.

3. The Committee considers that the two most urgent problems concern global warming and ozone depletion and it recommends that these should assume high priority within the construction industry.

Global Warming:

4. There are still many uncertainties concerning the acceleration of the greenhouse effect. However, the majority scientific opinion is that global warming is bound to occur even though there is no agreement as to its rate of acceleration or the point at which it may cross the threshold of no return. There is also wide agreement that there will be consequential climatic changes some of which could be catastrophic. More information will be available later in the year, following the publication of the international scientific investigation report into global warming. Meanwhile, the profession needs to be aware of the balance of probability and to be alive to its responsibilities in relation to environmental damage and global warming.

5. The main contributor to global warming is carbon dioxide (CO_2) and it is estimated that 50 per cent of atmospheric fossil CO_2 comes from buildings and related industries. Design decisions by the Architect can have considerable impact on this percentage.

RIBA practice documents should be amended to include the duty that all members seek to persuade their clients to permit use of environmentally benign materials and the employment of energy efficient specification and construction.

6. The RIBA therefore recommends its members to take the following action:

    i) as a starting point, refer to BS 8207 and the Energy Efficiency Office 'Best Practice' document;

    ii) specify insulation standards above the current regulations where appropriate;

    iii) specify low-energy, high efficiency plant, fittings and appliances;

    iv) employ up-to-date controls to ensure that a building responds appropriately to internal and external conditions;

    v) design in such a way that the building is appropriately orientated and is sensitive to natural features and microclimate;

    vi) specify timbers only from sustainable forests. In this connection, the updated Friends of the Earth 'Good Wood Manual' will be of considerable help.

7. However, it is acknowledged that the Architect's powers of persuasion are limited and that many clients will only adopt environmentally and energy conscious design if coerced by legislation. There is an urgent need for the Government to adopt an integrated energy policy which embraces all Departments of State within which legislation would be introduced and finance made available in the following areas;

    i) to ensure that the insulation standards set under the Building Regulations are raised well above the 1990 level and to link this change with air tightness associated with prescribed ventilation standards, and supported by a Government led education and training programme;

    ii) to provide substantial subsidy for retro-fit insulation linked to a national energy design advisory scheme;

    iii) to introduce minimum efficiency standards and labelling for plant and appliances;

iv) to require the privatised utilities to promote energy conservation and adopt least cost planning procedures as a condition
of their licence;

v) to make an initial subsidy available for the manufacture of low
energy fittings (eg. light bulbs) until production achieves
economy of scale;

vi) to introduce the mandatory energy-efficiency rating initially of
all new domestic buildings and in due course of public and
commercial buildings, together with an inventory of materials
used in construction. All new buildings should have a log book
as part of their legal documentation stating their energy rating
and the materials used in construction.

Ozone Depletion:

8. Cholrofluorocarbons (CFCs) are implicated in damage to the
ozone layer, the earth's barrier against ultra-violet radiation. The
possible consequences of this include increased risk of skin cancer
and global warming, leading to climatic changes and rising sea levels.
In the construction sector CFCs are used to 'blow' foamed
insulation products, as refrigerants in air-conditioning cooling
systems and in fire protection equipment, which together form a
significant proportion of UK usage of these chemicals. Eighty
countries, including the UK, agreed in the Helsinki Declaration
to phase out the production and consumption of CFCs as soon
as possible, but not later than the year 2000.

9. The following guidelines are therefore drawn to the attention of
members:

i) Avoid the use of CFC blown insulation. The materials
concerned include: polyurethane, polyisocyanurate and phenolic
foams; extruded polystyrene and aerosal sprayed foam
insulation.

ii) Use built forms, fenestration and construction that permit
natural or simple mechanical ventilation and thus minimise the
need for full air conditioning and associated refrigeration plant.

iii) If refrigeration plant is necessary, liaise with the building
services engineer to specify compliance with the CIBSE policy
on CFCs, which is summarised as follows: use refrigerant R22
until substitutes become available, as R22 has a relatively low
ozone-depletion potential; make adequate provision in the

design for the maintenance of systems to ensure long-term containment (leakage currently accounts for 50 to 75 per cent of refrigerant used); include access space for leak checking, detection alarms and regular inspection; require that refrigerant in refurbished or decommissioned plant is recycled.

iv) Where possible avoid the use of halon fire control systems as fire tests usually involve full-scale release of the gas. If the use of halon, a gas related to CFCs is absolutely necessary, investigate means of minimising leakage.

Future Agenda

10. In further pursuit of the above policies the EEPC will address the following issues:

i) hazardous materials, noxious substances and air quality;
ii) implications of life-cycle energy assessment;
iii) a co-ordinated environment/energy conscious approach to planning and transportation.

11. The EEPC will keep under review the design consequences of recommendations from such bodies as the International Panel on Climate Change involving large reductions in CO_2 emissions.

12. In addition the Committee will promote the publication of construction and specification details of energy efficient buildings from the United Kingdom and comparable climate zones.

Case Study: Codes of Practice

The Building Services Research and Information Association (BSRIA)/Construction Industry Research and Information Association (CIRIA) 'Environmental Code of Practice' is a recently published working document for designing green buildings, refurbishing buildings in an environmentally friendly way and minimising the environmental impact of buildings in use. Aimed primarily at buildings services engineers, it is also expected to be of use to architects, project managers and facilities staff.

Other codes of practice available include the Department of the Environment's *'Environmental Action Guide for Building and Purchasing Managers'* and *'Building for the Environment – An Environmental Good practice*

Checklist for the Construction and Development Industries', produced by the Leicester Environment City Trust.

Both the above also contain further lists of useful references and organisations to contact.

4   INTEGRATION METHODS

Both the Toyne Report and Agenda 21 suggest that cross-curricula environmental education should not be viewed as an optional extra tagged on to more traditional course material. Yet there are inherent difficulties in trying to remodel courses in their entirety along environmental lines.

It would be impossible to define a structure for the incorporation of environmental teaching into all built environment courses on a national scale. At least for the foreseeable future, it will fall to individual institutions to decide what constitutes valid environmental teaching and to try to integrate this into their existing courses.

The professional bodies have a role to play in extending their own environmental understanding in the workplace and in the influence that they have over accredited course content. Along with employers, the professional bodies need to ensure that vocational courses are continually updated to meet their own changing needs and that the environmental content covers as broad a base as possible.

Very few institutions have made progress in delivering environmental education outside traditional environmental studies courses. Schools and faculties in the built environment sector are better placed than most in this respect, particularly with regard to energy-related studies, but often lack the more global social dimensions associated with environmental studies in the spirit of Agenda 21.

The following section examines some of the approaches which could be used to integrate environmental material into courses.

4.1   Modular Approaches

Environmental modules may be optional or compulsory and generic or subject-specific. Each of these approaches has different merits.

Optional Modules

Optional modules are often available to students on a number of different courses. This allows themes of general environmental relevance to be explored and may be useful for encouraging personal responsibility towards the environment and the understanding of areas such as global climate change. However, where the environmental module is completely unrelated to the students' main areas of study, it may be difficult for them to make connections between the two. The environmental module may be seen as an interesting adjunct but irrelevant to the main field of study.

Compulsory Modules

Compulsory modules have the advantage that they can be planned to include material relevant to the main subject area. This would be comparatively easy in the built environment sector, where there are already obvious connections between the built and natural environments.

A compulsory module which is not completely customised can still hold advantages over the optional approach. So, for example, the same general environmental module could be compulsory for students from a number of different courses; minor alterations to the main subject modules would be agreed to emphasise the environmental connections. This might require collaboration between teaching staff in different departments.

The major problem with the introduction of compulsory modules is curriculum over-crowding. Introduction of an environmental module might mean the loss of another part of the course. The modular route can also be criticised as being fragmentary, making it difficult for students to make the links between personal and occupational environmental responsibility.

4.2   Alterations to the Syllabus

Another approach could involve the modification of all course elements to involve an environmental perspective. Such an approach might well meet with some resistance from staff, who would have to develop new course materials and may themselves not have much knowledge about environmental issues.

Within most sectors, including the built environment, the syllabus should undergo updating anyway, as legislation and practices change. Environmental material could then evolve into courses as outdated material is replaced. This is, however, a slow process.

4.3   Student Projects

Environmentally related projects are very useful as they allow students to investigate in depth the links between environmental and other aspects of their chosen topic. Chosen topic areas are also a good way of gauging student awareness and concern and create a demand for environmental resources within the institution. In the built environment, studies of the institution's own buildings can also be useful for institutional greening and environmental auditing purposes.

Student projects have the general advantage of developing life skills and working in partnership with potential employers and other organisations. In this way, environmentally oriented projects can have a general awareness-raising capacity.

Case Study: Environment and the Car – a Flexible Learning Resource developed by the University of Hertfordshire

This is a flexible learning resource pack, which could be used by students and teachers on a number of different courses, including architecture and planning. It contains readings from books, journals, newspaper articles and conference papers relating to transport trends, policy and control, environmental impact and solutions. The resource can be used to assist lecturers to integrate environmental principles and case studies into their courses or as a basis for developing a module. Students can use it for autonomous learning, group project work or to support course work.

4.4   Experiential Learning

This may include a number of options. For example, site visits to exhibitions, attendance at a public enquiry or visits to the Centre for Alternative Technology. In addition, work placements provide valuable experience. This would require finding suitably environmentally enlightened employers.

Field work is another option, as are competitions, for example the British Gas Energy Design Awards (the 1992 award was based on an idea for the design of a low-energy sixth-form college with shared community facilities).

The American Institute of Architects ran a competition called A Call for Sustainable Community Solutions. This had three categories of submissions and prizes: energy and resource efficiency; healthy buildings and materials; and land use and ecology.

The European Community also sponsored an architectural competition called Working in the City, which was concerned with the design of non-domestic buildings and aimed to promote passive design structures which are appropriate in an urban context and which take account of climate.

4.5   Environmental Learning Outcomes

Environmental learning outcomes are an expression of the level of environmental competence students are expected to achieve at the end of their course. In many employers' eyes, the development of broader graduate competences is more important than subject knowledge.[32] This includes the development of environmental competence. Using learning outcomes rather than the more traditional, process-related benchmarks of achievement (such as units attended) takes more account of prior learning and work-based experiences.

Environmental learning outcomes can be used in a self-contained way with each group of outcomes providing the basis for a module (either optional or compulsory). Alternatively, the same outcomes could be integrated within other modules. This approach is intended to allow close links to be made between sustainable concepts and the students' occupational interest, thereby improving student motivation.[33] There may be difficulties in assessing achievement in outcome-related courses.

5   EVALUATION METHODS

Cross-curricular greening is a relatively new area and as such methods for evaluating the true extent and depth of penetration of environmental teaching are still under development.

A series of performance indicators needs to be evolved which will examine:

- institutional commitment – policy, strategic plan, course review, staff appraisal, staff development programmes, conference attendance, corporate membership of environmental organisations;

- learning resources – key policy documents, open learning materials, journals, books;

- staff expertise and general awareness – qualifications, published papers and articles, voluntary work, subscription to environmental organisations;

- student access to environmental education – number of students who have the opportunity to set their chosen course in its appropriate environmental context, number of students who have the opportunity to examine the environmental impact of their own lifestyles;

- appropriate environmental content of curricula – accreditation by professional bodies, student evaluation of course, normal course review process, employer evaluation;

- environmental learning outcomes/environmental competence of students.

It should be noted that some environmental learning outcomes will be particularly difficult to evaluate. This applies especially to those dealing with personal responsibility towards the environment. There is very little evidence that can be produced to show that, for example, a learner is able to make personal decisions which take account of the environment.

In order to evaluate the progress of implementing institutional and curriculum greening, it is necessary to formulate a baseline. A review of current curriculum environmental content and staff attitudes can provide such a baseline. Regular curriculum auditing can then provide a measure of ongoing achievement.

A number of FHE institutions are now employing environmental policy officers to take on this task. At Northumbria University a one-year post has been created to look specifically at greening the curriculum.[34] Again, the role of the professional bodies must be stressed. Where a professional body has already produced an environmental policy or guidelines of its own, it should ensure that any courses it validates, accredits or examines meet those criteria.

Evaluation of student achievement is particularly difficult. Many of the desired results of cross-curricular greening are hard to define or intangible. Some examples are given in the BTEC Case Study as to possible performance criteria.

6 CONCLUSIONS

Built Environment faculties seem to concentrate their attention on energy and related matters at the expense of other environmental issues. Areas such as waste minimisation, alternative sources of materials and the use of non-harmful materials are not often covered. The kind of issues which are covered depends on the nature of the course, for example, planners are usually taught something about Environmental Impact Assessment (EIA) but architects may not be, even though many of the developers subject to EIA will be employing architects at some stage.

Issues related to the global environment (except global warming as an energy-related issue) and the interface between environment and development issues are most often absent. This may be because the built environment is associated with specific localities (towns and cities) and the wider implications of building materials, transport of goods, and transboundary pollution are not immediately apparent.

However, this situation is likely to change as courses become more tuned to the needs of sustainable development, based on the documents arising from the Earth Summit conference (UNCED) held in Rio de Janeiro in 1992. Agenda 21 (an agenda for the twenty-first century) includes a chapter on the needs for local decision-making to reflect the principles contained in the main document. This includes an increase in community participation in the decision-making process. Many local authorities in the UK are now putting together their own local Agenda 21 programmes and students should be encouraged to find out about this process in their own locality. Agenda 21 emphasises the need for an increase in the involvement of young people in determining environmental strategy, and students should also be made aware of this.

All Built Environment courses should include some element relating to the life-cycle of the goods and materials used and some element of the policy/decision-making process involved in deciding where and how developments take place, the form of construction and the overall planning behind the creation/regeneration of urban communities.

APPENDIX I – WORKSHOPS HELD AT THE BUILT ENVIRONMENT SEMINAR

A seminar was held at De Montfort University on 15 July 1993 to share experiences of various aspects of environmental education in the built environment sector and to discuss the original draft of this document. A number of practitioners from both FHE and the professions spoke or conducted workshops. A summary of the workshops' content is given below:

Workshop A – Environmental Education in the Workplace

Case study presenters: Sarah Hiscock (National Power's) Environmental
                         Policy Officer
                         Graham Pinfield (Lancashire County Council)

A company-wide environmental awareness programme was launched by National Power in January of this year [1993]. Sarah Hiscock provided an introductory outline of who and what National Power are and why they have initiated a company-wide environmental awareness programme. The workshop looked at how top level commitment was obtained to go ahead with the programme, how it was developed and the reasoning behind the approach, a brief description of what it contains, the training programme for presenters which underpins the programme, and progress so far.

Graham Pinfield has a degree in Environmental Biology and Geology and has just completed a master's degree in Environmental Planning. He has worked in urban nature conservation in Birmingham and London, moving on to environmental planning and policy work in Bedfordshire and now Lancashire. He helped compile the Lancashire and the Environment Staff Briefing Programme and has delivered the package to colleagues in the Planning Department.

Graham presented a case study on the Lancashire and the Environment Staff Briefing Programme which outlined the training strategy that has been devised and is now being implemented by Lancashire County Council as part of its internal environmental audit or 'Better Environmental Practices Strategy'. The aims and scope of the project were covered together with an outline of what the training programme consists of and how it was drawn up. The mechanism for delivering the programme to staff was detailed, together with feedback and lessons learned from the first round of training in the authority. The future development of the training programme rounded off the presentation.

Workshop B – The Role of the Professional Bodies

Case study presenters: Cliff Hague (RTPI)
                        Paul Murray (RICS)

Cliff Hague is Chair of the Professional Qualifications Committee of the Royal Town Planning Institute and a member of the institute's Council. He is Head of the School of Planning and Housing at Edinburgh College of Art/Heriott–Watt University. Cliff discussed how the environmental agenda in planning has expanded from one based on a conservation ethic to one based on sustainable development. The RTPI has three strands of education policy potentially affecting the treatment of the environment in higher education: education guidelines; CPD policy and research guidelines. His case study examined these guidelines and their effect on the accreditation of courses.

Paul Murray is a lecturer in the School of Civil and Structural Engineering at the University of Plymouth. He discussed the role of the Royal Institute of Chartered Surveyors in pursuing environmental education goals in higher education courses.

Workshop C – Curriculum Auditing

Case study presenter: Quentin Merritt (University of Central Lancashire)

Quentin Merritt was formerly the Environmental Officer of the University of Central Lancashire, and is now employed by the University of Greenwich.

He worked in Lancashire from October 1991, having been appointed to undertake an environmental review of the institution and to develop and help implement a programme of environmental improvements. He was then involved in coordinating efforts to introduce an environmental management system at the university, with a view to possible certification for the new British Standard (BS 7750). Quentin represented the university on the Education Working Group of the BS 7750 pilot programme and is a founder member of the Environmental Management and Environmental Auditing Research Network. Before joining the university he gained an MSc in Environmental Technology from Imperial

College, London, worked for an environmental consultancy and undertook air pollution research in Mexico City.

His presentation reviewed the environmental initiatives introduced at the University of Central Lancashire. These began with a policy statement in 1990 and the establishment of an Environmental Committee to advise on its implementation. The Environment Committee commissioned the Environmental Audit Project in 1991 and the follow-up Environmental Management Systems project in 1992. The university is currently in the process of introducing an EMS. It has been involved in the Pilot programme for the new British Standard BS 7750. At the same time there have been a number of practical initiatives including paper recycling, greening the campus and energy monitoring and target setting.

Workshop D – Embedding Green Issues 1

Case study presenter: Elizabeth Shove (University of Sunderland)

Dr Shove was previously employed as a research fellow at the Institute of Advanced Architectural Studies, University of York, and is now Senior Lecturer and Director of the Buildings and Society Research Unit at the University of Sunderland. She is a Sociologist with some six years experience of building research. Current work includes a major project 'Putting Science into Practice: Saving Energy in Buildings', funded by the Economic and Social Research Council's global environmental change programme. This study examines social, economic and organisational factors influencing the development of energy-related building research and the practical application of the resulting expertise.

Workshop E – Embedding Green Issues 2

Case study presenter: Shirley Ali Khan (University of Hertfordshire)

Shirley Ali Khan is currently the National Coordinator for Further and Higher Education for the Council for Environmental Education. She has written a number of publications on the subject of greening in higher education including *Colleges Going Green* (CPD, 1992) and *Greening the Curriculum* (CPD, 1991). Her most recent publication was the *BTEC Environmental Initiative* (BTEC, 1993). She was also an acknowledged contributor to the Department for Education Environmental Responsibility Report (1993).

Shirley is also a member of several national committees including the Local Government Management Board: Agenda 21 National Steering Committee, and the World Wide Fund for Nature: Education Committee. She is a director of the Environment Council.

Workshop F – Use of Practical Examples

Case study presenters: Roger Kelly (Centre for Alternative Technology)
Alan Hobbett (Leicester Eco-house)

Roger Kelly worked in the housing association movement and private practice before teaching at Hull and Bath schools of Architecture. He researched into the sustainability of rural settlements and ran an advisory service for rural small businesses before moving to Cyprus to become community architect and builder in a small village, combined with running environmental summer schools. He has been Director of the Centre for Alternative Technology since 1988.

Alan Hobbett is manager of the Leicester Eco-house. His presentation described the use of the Eco-house as a demonstration project and educational resource.

APPENDIX II – RESOURCES

The following examples illustrate some of the organisations which may be available to give help to FHE practitioners. A longer contact list and references are given in the final section of the booklet.

The Centre for Alternative Technology

Founded in 1974 and situated in mid-Wales, the Centre for Alternative Technology is a display and education centre offering practical ideas and information on environmentally sound practices. Displays included in the 40-acre site show examples of wind, water and solar power, low energy buildings and organic growing.

The centre runs over 100 residential courses each year for schools and FHE institutions, and a number of FHE institutions make regular visits to the centre. Students from a variety of disciplines attend, including architecture and engineering.

The courses aim to back up hard technical facts with workshops and discussions on the environmental and social implications of typical and alternative technologies. The lectures stimulate lateral thinking and stress the connections between different aspects of the centre's work. Courses are designed in cooperation with the FHE department concerned and are specifically adapted to the needs and abilities of the students. Thus the centre acts as a living example of how personal and professional values can come together to provide good environmental practice.

Construction Industry Research and Information Association (CIRIA)

CIRIA run an Environmental Forum, jointly with BRE (the Building Research Establishment) and BSRIA (Building Services Research and Information Association). Approximately 130 organisations subscribe to the initiative which provides a focus for all sectors of the construction and related industries to discuss environmental issues of concern. The forum's programme consists of regular discussion meetings and a programme of research-related projects.

Typical evening discussion meetings focus on topics such as: specifying and purchasing timber; nature conservation issues in building and construction; environmental issues in construction; waste management – duty of care; BSRIA Environmental Code of Practice; the environment existing in Offices – BRE; and life-cycle/eco-analysis. Regular bulletins are also sent out to members.

The Ecological Design Association (EDA)

The EDA links designers in a global network to provide information, education, exchange of ideas and stimulation for new design worldwide. The educational sub-committee consists of students and lecturers from universities and colleges and produces regular newsletters, including a page devoted to education issues.

The EDA promotes:

- the design of materials and products, projects and systems, environments and communities which are friendly to living species and planetary ecology;

- professional and consumer awareness of ecological design and informed choice;

- interdisciplinary contacts between architects, surveyors, interior designers, developers, product designers, engineers and technologists, building biologists, doctors and clinical ecologists, therapists, artists, manufacturers, contractors, marketeers and retailers, the public and the media;

- education and the involvement of young people to facilitate the spread of eco-design and the training of designers and innovators;

- research and evaluation and the setting of standards for ecological projects, services, materials and products.

REFERENCES

1. Toyne, P. (chair) (1993) 'Environmental Responsibility – An agenda for Further and Higher Education', Report of the Committee on Environmental Education in Further and Higher Education (HMSO).
2. Environmental Protection Act 1990,(1990) Part III S (74). HMSO.
3. United Nations Conference on Environment and Development, Agenda 21, Chapter 36. Advance copy, p. 5–7.
4. Elkin, T. and McLaren D. (1991) 'Reviving the City – Towards Sustainable Urban Development', Friends of the Earth, p. 12.
5. Snow, D. March 1993 RIBA Journal *Practice*, Issue 93, p. 1–3.
6. Birtles, T. *et. al* November 1992 'Planning for Energy Efficiency' in *The Planner*, p. 8.
7. British Aggregate Construction Materials Industry *Statistical Yearbook 1988* 1989 (London, BACMI).
8. Borer, P. *et al* (1992) *Environmental Building* (Powys: Centre for Alternative Technology).
9. ——. (1992) Environmental Building. (Powys: Centre for Alternative Technology).
10. Coles, T. *et al* (1992) 'Practical Experience of Environmental Assessment in the UK', paper to the Advances in Environmental Assessment Conference in October 1992 (IBC/IEA).
11. Halls, Dr S.A. (1992) 'The Environment and Planning: An Integrated Approach', paper to the Advances in Environmental Assessment Conference in October 1992 (IBC/IEA).
12. Wood, C. (1989) *Planning Pollution Prevention – Anticipatory Controls over Air Pollution Sources* (Heinemenn Newnes).
13. ENDS Report (1993) no. 219, p. 10.
14. Elkin, T. and McLaren D. (1991) 'Reviving the City – Towards Sustainable Urban Development', Friends of the Earth, p. 36.
15. Toyne, P. (chair) (1993) 'Environmental Responsibility – An Agenda for Further and Higher Education', Report of the Committee on Environmental Education in Further and Higher Education, p. 89 (HMSO).
16. Wilson, I. Chief Engineer DMU, personal communication.
17. BTEC Environmental Initiative (1993) 'Guidance for the Incorporation of Environmental Components into BTEC programmes'.
18. Vale, R. (September 1990) 'Energy and Environmental Teaching in the UK Schools of Architecture', report for the RIBA Environmental and Energy Committee.

19. Roaf, S. and Hanclock, M. (undated) *Assessing and Meeting the Needs in Energy and Environmental Education in the 1990s: The Situation in Britain.*

20. Roaf, S. and Hanclock, M. (undated) *Assessing and Meeting the Needs in Energy and Environmental Education in the 1990s: The Situation in Britain.*

21. Owen, G.W.P. (1992) 'Excellence, Quality & Corporate Environmentalism, the Vision, the mission and the MO', Article for KPH/GMI journal.

22. World Commission on Environment and Development (1986) *The Brundtland Report.*

23. ENDS Report November 1993 no. 226, p. 11.

24. ENDS Report April 1992 no. 207, p. 3.

25. ENDS Report March 1993 no. 218, p. 19.

26. ENDS Report January 1993 no. 216, p. 3.

27. Toyne, P. (chair) (1993) 'Environmental Responsibility – An agenda for Further and Higher Education', Report of the Committee on Environmental Education in Further and Higher Education, p. 86 (HMSO).

28. Toyne, P. (chair) (1993) 'Environmental Responsibility – An agenda for Further and Higher Education', Report of the Committee on Environmental Education in Further and Higher Education, p. 86 (HMSO).

29. European Parliament (1993–94 session) 'Resolution on the use of bioclimatic construction technology for residential and work premises', extract of the minutes of the meeting of 11/2/94.

30. RTPI (1991) 'The Education of Planners', policy statement and general guidance for academic institutions offering initial professional education in planning.

31. RIBA (1990) 'Initial Policy Statement on Global Warming and Ozone Depletion'.

32. Otter, S. (1993) 'Learning Outcomes: Issues in Course Delivery and Design', a conference for the staff of De Montfort University.

33. BTEC Environmental Initiative May 1993 'Guidance for the Incorporation of Environmental Components into BTEC Programmes'.

34. Mann, H. Environmental Policy Officer, Northumbria University, personal communication.

Atkinson, C. J. and Butlin, R. N. 'Ecolabelling of Building materials and Building Products', BRE Information Paper 11/93 (Building Research Establishment, 1993).

Baldwin, R., Bartlett, P., Leach, S. J. and Attenborough, M., BREEAM 4/43, 'An Environmental Assessment for Existing Office Buildings' (Building Research Establishment, 1993).

Barwise, J. and Battersby, S., *Environmental Training* (Croner Publications, 1993).

Bright, K., 'Building a Greener Future – Environmental Issues Facing the Construction Industry', CIOB Occasional Paper 49 (Chartered Institute of Building, 1991).

BS7750: 1992 Specification for Environmental Management Systems (BSI, London, 1992).

BS7750 2nd Edition Draft for Public Comment, DC400220/93 (BSI, London, 1993).

'CFCs in Buildings' BRE Digest 358, (Building Research Establishment 1992).

Butler, D. and Howard, P. N., 'Life Cycle CO_2 Emissions: From the Cradle to the Grave' in *Building Services*, 1992.

Butler, D., 'Guidance on the Phase–out of CFCs for Owners and Operators of Air Conditioning Systems', PD25/93 (Building Research Establishment, 1993).

Corporate Environmental Policy Statements (Confederation of British Industry, London, June 1992).

CIBSE, Building Energy Code, in 4 parts (CIBSE, 1975–82).

CIC Environmental Task Group, 'Our Land for Our Children: An Environmental Policy for the Construction Professions' (Construction Industry Council, August 1992).

CIEC Environment Task Force, 'Construction and the Environment' (BEC, May 1942).

'Climate and Site Development', BRE Digest 350 (Building Research Establishment 1990).

BIBLIOGRAPHY

Ali Khan S, 1992, *BTEC Environmental Initiative*, BTEC, London.

Ali Khan S, 1992, *Colleges Going Green: A Guide to Environmental Action in Further Education Colleges*, Further Education Unit, London.

Centre for Human Ecology, University of Edinburgh, 'Environmental Education for Adaptation', November 1991.

Committee of Directors of Polytechnics, 'Greening Polytechnics', October 1990.

Committee of Directors of Polytechnics, 'Greening the Curriculum', May 1991.

Committee of Vice Chancellors and Principals, 'Universities & the Environment: Environmental Regulation – Opportunities & Obligations', February 1992, ISBN 0 9488 19 3.

Department for Education, 1992, *Environmental Responsibility: An Agenda for Further and Higher Education*, HMSO, London.

Government White Paper on the Environment, 'Our Common Inheritance', HMSO, September 1990, ISBN 0 10 112002 8.

Institution of Environmental Sciences, *Environmental Education in Higher Education*, Position Paper, 1994.

National Curriculum Council, 'Environmental Education', *Curriculum Guidance* 7, 1990.

Scottish Environmental Education Council, 'Towards Environmental Competence in Scotland: An Overview', November 1991, ISBN 0 948773 12 X.